Bold Exit

Knowing When to Quit for a Better Tomorrow

By

Lane J. Taylor

Disclaimer

The information, views, and opinions expressed in this book, "Bold Exit: Knowing When to Quit for a Better Tomorrow," are solely those of the author and do not necessarily represent the views or opinions of any affiliated individuals, organizations, or entities.

The content of this book is intended for informational and educational purposes only. It is not a substitute for professional advice, guidance, or services. Readers are encouraged to consult with appropriate professionals in the relevant fields for personalized advice tailored to their specific situations.

The author and publisher make no representations or warranties of any kind, express or implied, regarding the completeness, accuracy, reliability, or suitability of the information provided within this book. Any reliance you place on such information is strictly at your own risk. The author and publisher disclaim any responsibility for any loss, injury, or damage resulting directly or indirectly from the use or application of the information presented in this book. Readers are encouraged to exercise their own judgment and seek the advice of qualified professionals when making decisions based on the content of this book.

The inclusion of external links or references in this book does not imply endorsement or approval of the content, products, or services provided by the linked sources. The author and publisher have no control over the nature, content, and availability of external sites or resources.

Every effort has been made to ensure that the information in this book is accurate at the time of publication. However, the author and publisher do not assume and hereby disclaim any liability to any party for any loss, damage, or disruption caused by errors or omissions, whether such errors or omissions result from negligence, accident, or any other cause.

This disclaimer is subject to change without notice, and it is the responsibility of readers to review and understand the most current version. By reading this book, readers acknowledge and agree to the terms of this disclaimer.

About the Author

Lane J. Taylor, the insightful author of "Bold Exit: Knowing When to Quit for a Better Tomorrow," brings a passion for exploring human decisions and resilience. With a background in psychology, Lane delves into the complexities of quitting, success, and the transformative power of letting go.

Through personal experiences and a commitment to lifelong learning, Lane's narrative reflects a nuanced understanding of the paradoxes of quitting, losses, and the intricacies of identity in pivotal decisions. "Bold Exit" is more than a book—it's Lane's personal reflection on the potential inherent in embracing change.

Inspired by Lane's encounters with forced quitting and the resilience gained, the book is an empathetic guide toward a more authentic future. Lane J. Taylor invites readers to connect with insights on self-discovery, resilience, and the courage to make strategic decisions for a better tomorrow.

Table of contents

Introduction

Step into a world where the norm is challenged, where "Bold Exit: Knowing When to Quit for a Better Tomorrow" isn't just about quitting—it's an exploration of the strategic art of making exits that redefine your journey. We're about to navigate the subtle nuances that go against the grain, discovering the unexpected virtue in knowing when to let go.

Our journey begins with a paradox: realizing that the opposite of great virtue is, indeed, another form of greatness. We're diving deep into the psyche of quitting, wrestling with the tough question of whether leaving is an act of weakness or a smart move towards personal and professional growth. The struggle unfolds as we explore the delicate dance between sticking it out and recognizing the opportune moment to walk away. As we turn the pages, we unravel the intricacies of losses. We shine a light on the pitfalls of escalating commitment, the weight of sunk costs, and the emotional baggage that clings to us in the form of metaphorical "monkeys and pedestals." The narrative expands to reveal the dynamics of ownership—not just of tangible possessions but also of our thoughts and beliefs. We face the challenge of quitting when it feels like our identity is on the line, discovering profound insights about finding love without the weight of hurt feelings.

The journey continues, delving into the core of personal identity. We confront the difficulty in quitting who we are and navigate the emotional labyrinth tied to self-identity. Love without attachment becomes a delicate balance, exploring relationships where caring is unconditional, yet not burdened by emotional baggage.

Moving forward, we draw inspiration from stories of forced quitting, understanding the resilience and growth that can emerge from situations where quitting is not a choice but a necessity. We then confront the narrow focus of goals, acknowledging the concept of opportunity cost in our pursuit of success and recognizing the hindrance that narrow aspirations can pose to long-term fulfillment.

Redefining success becomes a pivotal theme, challenging preconceived notions and celebrating the liberating power of letting go for a brighter future. Embracing change emerges as a transformative force for personal and professional growth, with poignant narratives of individuals finding success through bold exits.

This is not just a story of quitting; it's an invitation to make bold exits, navigating the delicate dance between perseverance and the courage to step into a brighter future. Welcome to a journey that encourages not just quitting but embracing change with the hope of a better tomorrow.

Chapter 1

The Paradox of Quitting

Think about life like this intricate tapestry full of paradoxes. There's this fascinating idea that the opposite of what we usually consider a great virtue can also be, in its own way, a great virtue. It's like peeling back the layers of complexity that make up the human experience. Imagine a landscape where resilience and surrender aren't opposites but dance together. It's a place where strength doesn't always come from holding on but sometimes emerges from vulnerability. And in this setting, the seemingly simple act of letting go becomes a profound act of courage – stepping into the unknown with an open heart.

Let me tell you about Jenna, a go-getter entrepreneur. She held onto her dreams with an iron grip, a virtue applauded by everyone around her. But when life threw curveballs, making her path seem like a dead-end street, she discovered a different kind of strength in considering a U-turn. That shift from unwavering persistence to strategic quitting turned out to be her ticket to unexpected success.

Now, think about Winston Churchill. His wartime persistence was legendary – a great virtue indeed. Yet, after the war, he gracefully transitioned into advocating for peace, showcasing the virtue of adapting to changing circumstances. It's like saying the same person can embody different virtues at different times.

Relationships, too, have their tales. Mark and Lisa were the epitome of commitment, sharing a history that defined their bond. But as individual dreams evolved, their commitment took on a new form – the courage to acknowledge that paths can diverge. In releasing the old, they found room for personal growth and the potential for a different, yet equally virtuous, connection. This concept isn't just a historical phenomenon; it's part of everyday life. It's knowing when to persist and when to gracefully let go. It's understanding that virtue isn't a fixed destination but a journey that requires us to navigate the twists and turns with grace. It's like saying, "Hey, I'll persist when it serves me well, but I'll also recognize when it's time to shift gears." In this paradox, we discover the core of human resilience – the ability to adapt, evolve, and sometimes, redefine what it means to be great. It's acknowledging that the path to virtue isn't a straight line but a dance, where recognizing the opposite virtue might just hold the key to a richer, more fulfilling life.

Now let's talk about Quitting on time and Quitting too early, The internal struggle between quitting on time and the fear of quitting too early delves into human decision-making complexity. This narrative, echoing the universal challenge of balancing perseverance and strategic exits, unfolds in scenarios like jobs, projects, or relationships. As initial enthusiasm wanes amid mounting obstacles, the conflict arises when contemplating timely quitting for well-being and long-term success. Yet, rational considerations clash with the emotional fear of quitting prematurely, rooted in societal norms that glorify persistence. This internal struggle involves acknowledging diminishing returns, battling anxieties about societal perceptions, and navigating emotional turmoil. Quitting on time becomes a multidimensional process, requiring a profound examination of personal beliefs amid changing circumstances.

Let me share a story about Rachel, a seasoned project manager, and her internal battle between quitting on time and the nagging feeling that it might be quitting too early. Rachel was known for her unwavering commitment, a trait that had defined her professional journey. Early in her career, she encountered a challenging project that demanded her expertise, time, and energy.

As the project faced unexpected hurdles, Rachel found herself at a crossroads. On one side, there was the pressure to persist – a commitment ingrained in her professional ethos. Completing the project had become more than a goal; it was a testament to her capabilities and resilience. This internal narrative echoed societal expectations where perseverance was celebrated as a virtue.

However, as challenges persisted, signs of burnout emerged, and the project's trajectory seemed to plateau. The internal conflict heightened. Quitting on time, considering a strategic exit, became a means of self-preservation and long-term success. Yet, the fear of quitting too early cast a shadow. Would leaving prematurely be seen as a lack of dedication? Would it undermine her professional reputation?

The emotional turmoil intensified as Rachel grappled with the decision. The fear of societal judgment, coupled with her belief in the virtue of persistence, created a formidable barrier to considering an early exit. It wasn't just a professional dilemma but a deeply personal one, entwined with questions of identity, self-worth, and the pursuit of excellence.

In this internal struggle, the concept of "quitting on time" revealed its complexity. It wasn't merely about chronological timing but a dance between recognizing diminishing returns, acknowledging personal well-being, and overcoming societal conditioning that glorifies unwavering persistence. The fear of quitting too early, a perceived misstep in the eyes of others, added layers of doubt and hesitation.

Rachel's journey mirrors a broader societal narrative that often celebrates resilience at the expense of well-being. The workplace culture, ingrained with the idea that quitting equals failure, contributed to her internal conflict. The fear of being labeled as someone who gives up easily haunted her, making it challenging to embrace the possibility that quitting on time could be a strategic move towards a promising future.

As Rachel navigated this internal conflict, seeking guidance and reflecting on her values, she began to recognize the importance of reframing the narrative. Quitting on time, far from being a sign of weakness, became an act of courage and strategic foresight. It was about reclaiming agency over her professional trajectory, acknowledging that the pursuit of excellence sometimes requires the wisdom to step back, reassess, and strategically choose the path forward.

The resolution of Rachel's internal conflict unfolded as she made the decision to strategically exit the challenging project. Contrary to her initial fears, this move did not tarnish her professional reputation; instead, it opened doors to new opportunities. Rachel's story became a testament to the transformative power of recognizing when to quit on time, embracing change, and prioritizing well-being without succumbing to the perpetual fear of quitting too early.

In essence, this exploration of the internal conflict illuminates a broader societal conversation about the narratives we construct around persistence and quitting. It challenges the notion that quitting is synonymous with failure and encourages a nuanced understanding that strategic exits can be profound acts of courage, wisdom, and self-preservation. It invites individuals and organizations to reevaluate their perspectives on quitting, fostering a culture that values both perseverance and the strategic wisdom to quit on time for a better tomorrow.

Chapter 2

Psychological Struggle in Decision-Making

The perennial question, "Should I stay or should I go?" encapsulates a psychological struggle that resonates across various facets of human experience. This internal dialogue unfolds in relationships, careers, personal endeavors, and other life junctures, highlighting the intricate nature of decision-making. Analyzing this struggle delves into the depths of human psychology, exploring the factors that contribute to the dilemma, the cognitive processes at play, and the emotional rollercoaster that often accompanies such decisions.

At the core of the "stay or go" dilemma lies the initial seed of doubt. This seed, inconspicuous at first, germinates from dissatisfaction, external pressures, or a yearning for change. It begins to sprout, taking root in the individual's consciousness, setting the stage for a psychological conflict that demands introspection. The decision to stay or go is rarely binary; it exists on a spectrum nuanced with uncertainty, fear, and hope. Individuals find themselves navigating this spectrum, grappling with the consequences and benefits each option presents. The internal weighing of pros and cons becomes a mental calculus, an attempt to foresee the potential outcomes of either choice.

Also Emotions, powerful and sometimes unpredictable, play a pivotal role in decision-making. The psychological struggle intensifies as conflicting emotions surface – fear of the unknown, attachment to the familiar, excitement for new possibilities, and anxiety about potential regrets. Navigating this emotional terrain becomes a delicate dance, as individuals try to discern which feelings hold genuine significance. Decision-making is intricately tied to cognitive processes, and the "stay or go" dilemma is no exception. The mind engages in a continuous process of evaluation, drawing on memories, experiences, and anticipations. Cognitive biases may come into play, coloring perceptions and influencing the perceived risks and benefits associated with each choice.

In the realm of attachment and comfort, staying often provides a sense of security rooted in the familiar. Human beings are creatures of habit, finding comfort in routines, relationships, and environments that have become integral parts of their lives. The psychological allure of maintaining the status quo stems from this intrinsic need for stability. The prospect of leaving behind what is known and venturing into the unknown is a formidable psychological hurdle. Fear of change, fueled by uncertainties about the future, can create a powerful resistance to the idea of going. The mind grapples with the imagined challenges and disruptions associated with stepping out of the comfort zone. The psychological concept of the sunk cost fallacy often surfaces in decisions about staying. Individuals may rationalize their choice by considering the investments they've made – be it in a relationship, a job, or a project – as reasons to persist. The idea of "I've invested so much; I can't quit now" becomes a mental anchor, sometimes preventing an objective evaluation of the present situation.

In the urge for growth and change, the human spirit has an inherent desire for growth and self-improvement. The psychological struggle to stay or go can be fueled by a yearning for new experiences, challenges, and opportunities that foster personal development. This realm represents the quest for a more fulfilling and meaningful life. The call of the unknown, with its promise of adventure and potential rewards, can be enticing. Individuals contemplating leaving may experience a psychological pull toward unexplored horizons, driven by the belief that true personal and professional fulfillment lies beyond the current confines.

The fear of regret can be a powerful psychological force. The prospect of looking back and wondering "What if?" haunts decision-makers. This fear, rooted in the anticipation of future remorse, can sway the decision-making process, prompting individuals to lean towards staying to avoid potential regret.

In stories that unfold in the real world, consider the case of a couple, Alex and Sarah, facing the decision of whether to stay in their comfortable yet stagnant relationship or venture into the unknown. For Alex, the familiarity of the routine and shared history was a source of emotional security. The fear of dismantling what they had built over the years became a significant psychological barrier to considering the option of going. The psychological struggle was palpable in Alex and Sarah's relationship. Alex found solace in the routine, despite a growing sense of unfulfillment. The fear of change, coupled with a sense of obligation to the shared history, created a psychological conflict that echoed through their conversations and moments of introspection. The decision to stay was not solely based on the tangible elements of the relationship; it was deeply entwined with the psychological comfort derived from familiarity. The struggle involved untangling the emotional attachment to routine and questioning whether the perceived security was worth sacrificing personal growth and happiness.

The decision-making process, a psychological kaleidoscope, involves evaluating the present, anticipating the future, and navigating social and cultural influences. Intuition becomes a guiding force, and the power of choice emerges as a triumph. Embracing change becomes a psychological resilience, and the entire journey becomes a profound learning experience.

In the labyrinth of "should I stay or should I go," individuals embark on a psychological odyssey that unfolds in the realms of attachment, comfort, growth, and change. This internal struggle, laden with emotions, cognitive evaluations, and societal influences, epitomizes the complexity of human decision-making.

The decision to stay or go is not just a question; it is a psychological exploration, a journey into the depths of the human psyche. This odyssey, though challenging, offers individuals the opportunity to understand themselves more deeply, embrace change courageously, and navigate the complexities of decision-making with resilience and insight. At its core, the psychological struggle of decision making is a testament to the power of choice. Decision-makers navigate through a myriad of emotions, cognitive evaluations, and external pressures to arrive at a decision that aligns with their authentic selves. The act of choosing becomes a psychological triumph, regardless of the chosen path.

The decision to go represents a psychological resilience to confront uncertainties. It signifies an acknowledgment that growth, both personal and professional, often resides outside the comfort zone. This resilience becomes a psychological muscle, honed through the struggle, that empowers individuals to face the challenges inherent in change. The psychological struggle itself becomes a profound learning experience. Regardless of the chosen path, the introspection, emotional navigation, and cognitive evaluations contribute to personal growth. Decision-makers glean insights about themselves, their values, and their capacity for resilience through the intricate dance of decision-making.

In the end, "should I stay or should I go" is not just a question; it is a psychological exploration, a journey into the depths of the human psyche.

The odyssey, though challenging, offers individuals the opportunity to understand themselves more deeply, embrace change courageously, and navigate the complexities of decision-making with resilience and insight.

Chapter 3

The Psychology of Losses

When we talk about understanding when to quit, it's like peeling back the layers of a decision-making onion. One crucial layer in this process is the concept of escalating commitment – a fancy term for that tendency we all have to keep going down a path, even when it's clear it's not leading anywhere good. Imagine you're working on a project, pouring your time, energy, and maybe even a bit of your soul into it. Escalating commitment is like this invisible force that makes you want to keep going, no matter what. Why? Well, it's partly because of something called the sunk cost fallacy. This is where you start factoring in all the resources you've already invested, like time and effort, and it messes with your ability to see things objectively. The more you've put in, the harder it is to walk away. But it's not just about the numbers; it's also about emotions. As you invest more, you become emotionally attached to what you're doing. Whether it's a project, a job, or a relationship, you start seeing it as a part of who you are. Quitting then feels like losing a piece of yourself. It's like trying to detach a sticker that's been stuck for way too long – it leaves a mark.

And then there's the fear of failure. Society has this weird way of making quitting sound like a four-letter word. We're told to persist, never give up, and all that motivational jazz. This fear of being labeled a quitter can mess with your head. It overrides the logical part of your brain that's saying, "Hey, maybe it's time to rethink this." But here's the thing – understanding when to quit doesn't mean you lack perseverance. It's not about giving up at the first sign of trouble. It's about being smart and recognizing when that persistence is turning into blind stubbornness. Quitting strategically is a skill – it's about knowing when the costs of staying on a sinking ship outweigh the potential benefits.

Think of it like this: successful entrepreneurs often talk about knowing when to pivot or quit a failing venture. They get that quitting one thing can open the door to something better. It's not about weakness; it's about adaptability. It's about saying, "Okay, this isn't working. Let's redirect our efforts to something more promising."

And let's not forget the idea of opportunity cost. It's like asking, "What could I be gaining by sticking with this versus trying something else?" If you're in a job that doesn't align with your passions or goals, staying because you've invested time doesn't just cost you time – it costs you the chance to explore more fulfilling opportunities.

So, understanding the dynamics of escalating commitment is like putting on glasses that help you see through the fog of persistence for persistence's sake. It's about recognizing the emotional ties, seeing through the fear of being labeled a quitter, and understanding that, sometimes, quitting strategically is the wisest move.

Alright, let's continue our journey through the tangled web of decision-making, this time focusing on two formidable foes: sunk costs and the fear of waste. These two culprits have a knack for hijacking our rational thinking, influencing choices, and making the decision-making process a bit of a psychological maze.

Sunk Costs: The Ghosts of Investments Past
Ever find yourself thinking, "Well, I've already invested so much time, money, or effort into this, I can't just walk away now"? Welcome to the realm of sunk costs. This sneaky cognitive bias tricks us into factoring in all the resources we've already poured into something, even if it's as futile as trying to revive a wilted plant.

Picture this: you've been working on a project that's starting to resemble a sinking ship. The more you invest – be it hours, creativity, or even tears – the harder it becomes to cut your losses and move on. Why? Because those sunk costs, the ones you can never get back, start clouding your judgment. It's like being on a doomed expedition and thinking, "Well, we've come this far; might as well keep going." But here's the kicker: those sunk costs are gone. Irretrievable. Considering them in your decision-making only adds unnecessary weight to the sinking ship, making it harder to swim to shore. It's like hauling around a backpack filled with bricks when you should be shedding the load and finding a lifeboat.

The Fear of Waste: A Dreaded Companion
Now, let's invite the fear of waste to the decision-making party. This fear whispers in your ear, "If you quit now, all that time and effort will be wasted. You'll have nothing to show for it." It's the dread of looking back and thinking, "What was the point of all that if I'm just going to walk away now?"
Imagine you've been in a job that's slowly draining the life out of you. The fear of waste

might convince you that if you quit, all those years of hard work will be for nothing. It's like being stuck in a bad movie and thinking, "I've invested an hour already; might as well suffer through the rest."

But here's the reality check: the time and effort you've spent are already gone, regardless of your next move. Staying in a situation solely to avoid the feeling of wasted effort is like throwing good time after bad. It's akin to finishing a terrible movie just because you've already endured half of it – a classic case of the fear of waste holding you hostage.

So, how do you break free from the clutches of sunk costs and the fear of waste?

First, recognize sunk costs for what they are – ghosts of investments past that shouldn't dictate your future. If the current path isn't leading where you want, don't let the weight of sunk costs anchor you down.

Second, confront the fear of waste head-on. Understand that quitting strategically isn't a waste; it's a recalibration. Your past efforts were stepping stones, not wasted moments. It's about redirecting your energy toward endeavors that align with your goals and well-being.

When you untangle yourself from these psychological knots, you liberate your decision-making. It becomes less about salvaging sinking ships and more about navigating towards new horizons.

Monkeys and Pedestals that Hinder Progress

Let's embark on a journey into the metaphorical landscape of "monkeys and pedestals" that often lurk in the shadows, impeding our progress and hindering our ability to move forward. This imaginative duo represents psychological barriers that, when left unexamined, can turn into formidable obstacles on the path to personal and professional growth.

Imagine carrying a backpack filled not with tools for your journey but with mischievous monkeys. These monkeys symbolize the unnecessary burdens we sometimes hoist onto our shoulders – worries, doubts, or outdated beliefs that cling to us like persistent shadows.

One monkey might represent the fear of failure, whispering in your ear that every step forward is a precarious venture. Another might embody imposter syndrome, convincing you that you don't belong on the path you've chosen. These monkeys are sly, disguising themselves as reasons for caution while secretly holding you back.

The challenge lies in recognizing these monkeys for what they are – illusions that hinder progress. Unraveling their grip involves a conscious effort to inspect each one, questioning their legitimacy and shedding the weight they impose. It's about freeing yourself from unnecessary doubts and fears that have overstayed their welcome.

Now, picture pedestals, lofty platforms where we place our ideals, aspirations, and sometimes, impossible standards of perfection. These pedestals can be deceptive, creating an illusion that reaching such heights is the only measure of success.

Placing an unattainable goal on a pedestal sets the stage for frustration and self-doubt. It's like gazing up at a peak so high that the very thought of climbing becomes overwhelming. Whether it's achieving a flawless project, maintaining an impeccable image, or constantly exceeding expectations, these pedestals create a perpetual cycle of discontent.

To unravel the pedestals hindering progress, it's essential to reassess the standards we've set for ourselves. Are these goals realistic? Do they allow room for growth and learning? Challenging oneself is admirable, but pedestals of perfection often do more harm than good. It's about lowering the pedestals, allowing for a journey that embraces both successes and failures as essential components of progress.

The process of unraveling "monkeys and pedestals" requires introspection and a willingness to challenge ingrained beliefs. It's about examining the monkeys on your back – those persistent worries and doubts – and acknowledging that they are not integral parts of your identity. You have the power to release them. Simultaneously, it involves inspecting the pedestals you've erected – those unattainable standards. Are they genuine markers of success, or are they illusory obstacles? Liberating progress from these constraints requires setting realistic goals, embracing the journey, and understanding that imperfection is not a hindrance but a testament to growth.

So when you unraveling these metaphorical hindrances, you pave the way for a more liberated and authentic progression. It's about acknowledging that progress isn't always a linear ascent; it's a dynamic journey with twists, turns, and occasional detours. In letting go of unnecessary burdens and unattainable ideals, you open the door to a path where genuine growth and fulfillment can flourish.

Chapter 4

Unveiling Ownership

In the journey of discerning when to quit for a better tomorrow, the mantra "You own what you have bought and what you have thought" becomes a profound guide, unraveling the intricate dynamics between ownership, attachment, and the pivotal decisions that shape our lives.

Material possessions often transcend their physical form, intertwining with our emotional identity. In the pursuit of a brighter future, the challenge arises when these possessions morph into anchors, tethering us to a status quo that may no longer serve our well-being. The reluctance to strategically quit can stem from a fear of losing not just possessions but facets of our identity woven into them. This exploration prompts a reevaluation of the emotional ties we have with our belongings, challenging us to consider the transformative potential of letting go.

Beyond physical belongings, the ownership of thoughts and beliefs shapes the narrative of our lives. As we contemplate strategic quitting, the resistance often emerges from the intricate relationship between our thoughts and our sense of self. Letting go of long-held beliefs can feel like abandoning a part of our identity. This exploration encourages a deeper understanding, emphasizing that strategic quitting is not a betrayal of who we are but a courageous step towards a future aligned with our evolving selves.

At its core, the journey toward a better tomorrow involves navigating the delicate balance between ownership and liberation. It prompts us to question the assumption that quitting equates to loss and challenges us to see quitting as a deliberate act of self-preservation and growth. Strategic detachment, both from material possessions and ingrained thoughts, becomes the key to unlocking a path that leads not only to a better tomorrow but to a more intentional and fulfilling future.

So, "You own what you have bought and what you have thought" emerges as a guiding principle in the art of strategic quitting. It invites us to reassess our attachments, to question the narratives surrounding our possessions and thoughts, and to embrace the liberating potential inherent in the conscious decision to quit for a better tomorrow.

Let's dive into a real tough spot we often find ourselves in when we're thinking about quitting – the part where it feels like we're tossing away a chunk of who we are. Picture this: our belongings, they're not just things, right? They're like markers of our identity. Now, imagine quitting and it feels like we're not just letting go of possessions; it's as if we're saying goodbye to a piece of ourselves. It's like closing a chapter that's been a defining part of our story. This emotional weight tied to what we own can make quitting seem like we're losing not just stuff, but a part of who we've become.

Now, think about beliefs and goals. We hold onto them tightly because they've become threads woven into our identity. Quitting in this realm isn't just a change of direction; it feels like we're rewriting our entire story. The challenge is figuring out how to shift gears without feeling like we're losing a core part of ourselves – the identity we've built around our beliefs and dreams.

But here's the real deal: quitting isn't a deletion of who we are; it's more like an upgrade to a better version of ourselves. It's about realizing that our identity isn't some fixed thing; it's a canvas we're constantly painting and repainting with the choices we make.

In essence, in the grand storyline of our journey, the tough part about quitting when it feels like a slice of our identity is on the line? That's a crucial plot twist. It's like this call to find that sweet spot between honoring who we've been and making space for the awesome person we're growing into. Strategic quitting, when faced with this challenge, is like this dance – preserving the core of who we are while leaving room for the growth and transformation that a better tomorrow promises.

Chapter 5

The Identity Struggle

Let's venture into the heart of a profound truth – the hardest thing to quit is who you are. This exploration takes us deep into the intricate layers of self-identity, unraveling the complexities that make the notion of quitting one's own essence such a formidable challenge.

Think about it – who we are isn't just a static state; it's a dynamic tapestry woven by our experiences, beliefs, and relationships. Quitting becomes a formidable task when it feels like we're letting go of not just habits or roles but a fundamental part of ourselves.

Consider the person who's defined by a career they've invested years into. Quitting that job isn't just a professional transition; it's a profound shift in self-identity. The fear isn't just about losing a title; it's about redefining who they are without it. On a personal level, the challenge intensifies when we confront aspects of our identity that are deeply ingrained – the patterns of behavior, thought processes, or even relationships that have become integral to who we perceive ourselves to be. Quitting these aspects feels like dismantling the very foundation of our identity, a process that can be unsettling and, at times, downright painful.

Yet, within this challenge lies a paradox. While the hardest thing to quit is who you are, it's also a gateway to profound personal transformation. It calls for a delicate balance between honoring the essence of who you've become and allowing space for the evolution of your identity. The journey into the intricacies of self-identity and quitting is not a linear one. It's a dance between holding onto the core elements that make you "you" and bravely stepping into the unknown spaces that beckon growth. It's about understanding that quitting certain aspects of yourself isn't a negation of your identity but a courageous act of self-redefinition.

Now let's talk about embarking on a journey to navigate the emotional rollercoaster tied to personal identity is no small feat, but here's a human-centric guide to help you through:

Reflect on Yourself: Take a moment to look within. Explore the various layers that make up your identity – the roles you play, the beliefs you hold, and the values that drive you. Understanding your identity sets the stage for a more intentional exploration.

Embrace Change: Your personal identity is like a living, breathing entity that evolves over time. Embrace the idea that quitting certain aspects of it doesn't mean losing a part of yourself; rather, it's an invitation for growth and self-renewal.

Be Mindfully Aware: Cultivate a mindful awareness of your emotions as you navigate changes. Whether it's fear, excitement, or uncertainty, let yourself feel without judgment. Mindfulness provides a space for clarity amid emotional complexity.

Align with Your Values: Check if the changes align with your core values. Ensuring authenticity in these shifts provides a solid foundation for navigating changes without losing your sense of integrity.

Take Small Steps: Rome wasn't built in a day, and neither is personal transformation. Consider making changes through small, incremental steps. This gradual approach helps you test the waters and adjust as needed.

Seek Support: Don't go it alone. Engage with friends, family, or mentors who understand your journey. Sharing your thoughts and feelings with supportive allies provides valuable perspectives and emotional sustenance.

Build Resilience: Acknowledge that change brings challenges. Cultivate resilience by viewing challenges as opportunities for learning and growth. Embrace the discomfort as part of the human experience.

Be Compassionate: Throughout the process, be kind to yourself. Understand that identity shifts are intricate, and you might encounter moments of uncertainty or setbacks. Embrace imperfection as a natural part of the journey.

Envision Your Future: Picture the future version of yourself that you aspire to become.

Create a positive vision aligned with your goals and values. This forward-looking perspective can be a motivating force during moments of doubt.

Chapter 6

Love Without Attachment

In the intricate tapestry of relationships, there exists a profound concept that resonates deeply – finding someone who not only loves you but possesses the ability to navigate decisions with a clarity unclouded by the often tumultuous sea of emotions. It's a delicate balance, an art form that holds immense significance both in our personal lives and within the complex dynamics of professional relationships.

Discovering a person who loves you profoundly is undoubtedly a treasure. Emotional connections weave the fabric of our relationships, providing a sense of support, understanding, and an unspoken bond that adds richness to our shared experiences. These emotional ties create the foundation of intimacy and belonging, fostering a connection that transcends the mundane.

Yet, within the warmth of emotional connections lies a subtle challenge – the need to balance these sentiments with the rationality demanded by objective decision-making. It's an acknowledgment that decisions, be they in matters of the heart or the boardroom, often benefit from a clear, unbiased perspective. While emotions offer valuable insights, allowing them to be the sole compass risks steering decisions solely based on sentiment, potentially compromising the pursuit of optimal outcomes. In this delicate dance, the realization surfaces that objective decisions may, at times, result in hurt feelings. It's not a dismissal of emotions but an acceptance that decisions, even when made with the utmost care and consideration, might not always align seamlessly with everyone's expectations. It's about creating a space where hurt feelings are acknowledged and validated, fostering an environment of open communication.

The essence of this concept extends beyond individual decisions to encompass the mutual growth and understanding inherent in relationships. Both partners contribute not only emotional support but also the willingness to challenge one another for personal and collective development. This dynamic interplay ensures that decisions are driven by a shared vision, a commitment to growth, and a deep understanding of each other's evolving needs. Striking the delicate balance between emotional connection and objective decision-making necessitates a foundation of open communication, mutual respect, and a shared commitment to growth. It's about fostering an environment where hurt feelings are acknowledged as part of the human experience, yet decisions are made with a clear understanding of the broader context and long-term goals.

In essence, the concept of finding someone who loves you while maintaining objectivity in decision-making is a testament to the maturity and depth of a relationship. It involves navigating the nuanced dance between emotions and reason, where emotional bonds fortify the connection, and objective decision-making ensures that the relationship thrives with purpose, resilience, and a shared vision for the future.

Chapter 7

The Myopia of Goals

In the dynamic pursuit of our goals, the concept of opportunity cost emerges as a silent yet influential force, guiding our decision-making and shaping the trajectory of our aspirations. Opportunity cost, in essence, embodies the trade-offs we inevitably face when making choices, urging us to consider not only what we gain but also what we forgo in the pursuit of our objectives.

At the heart of this concept lies the recognition that time, perhaps our most precious resource, carries an inherent opportunity cost. Every moment invested in a particular goal is a moment not spent on an alternative endeavor. Whether it's advancing a career, pursuing education, or cultivating personal development, understanding the opportunity cost prompts a thoughtful evaluation of the broader possibilities that could have been explored.

Opportunity cost encourages a nuanced approach to goal-setting. It compels us to balance the immediate gains of a chosen path with the long-term vision we aspire to achieve. By acknowledging the potential sacrifices inherent in our decisions, we become more intentional architects of our goals, striving for a harmonious blend of short-term achievements and enduring fulfillment.

In the pursuit of goals, the concept of opportunity cost serves as a compass for strategic decision-making. It pushes us beyond a narrow focus on singular objectives and prompts a holistic consideration of the choices before us. This broader perspective enables us to make decisions aligned not only with immediate aspirations but also with the overarching narrative of our life's journey. In situations where circumstances necessitate a pivot or forced quitting, opportunity cost takes on added significance. It becomes a teacher, offering valuable insights into the consequences of our choices. Forced quitting, viewed through the lens of opportunity cost, becomes a reflective exercise, guiding us to reassess our priorities, learn from experiences, and make more informed decisions in the continuous pursuit of our goals.

Furthermore, opportunity cost challenges the myopia often associated with goal-setting. Rather than fixating solely on the endpoint, it encourages us to broaden our perspective. By acknowledging the trade-offs involved, we can ensure that our pursuit aligns not only with specific goals but also with the holistic vision of the life we aim to lead.

So, opportunity cost is an ever-present companion in the journey of goal attainment. It invites us to be conscious stewards of our choices, recognizing that each decision carries not only the promise of achievement but also the weight of what could have been.

Let's talk about myopic goals – those goals that are so narrowly focused on the immediate outcome that they often hinder decision-making and long-term success. It's like wearing blinders that limit our perspective, preventing us from seeing the broader landscape of possibilities and potential pitfalls.

When our goals become myopic, it's akin to looking through a narrow tunnel. We get fixated on a specific endpoint, and while that can provide a clear direction, it also blinds us to the nuanced choices and opportunities that exist beyond our immediate target. This tunnel vision can restrict our ability to make well-rounded decisions.

Myopic goals tend to encourage decisions made in isolation, narrowly tailored to achieve the immediate objective. Without considering the broader context, these decisions may not align with our long-term vision, potentially leading to unintended consequences or missed opportunities for growth.

Remember our companion, opportunity cost? Myopic goals often overlook this crucial aspect. They might prioritize short-term gains without weighing the potential trade-offs and sacrifices involved. This oversight can limit our ability to make informed decisions that align with our overall life narrative.

Goals with a myopic focus can stifle adaptability. Life is dynamic, and circumstances change. When our goals are inflexible, it becomes challenging to pivot when needed. This lack of adaptability can hinder our ability to navigate unexpected challenges and seize new opportunities that may lead to long-term success. Building on the wisdom of opportunity cost, myopic goals can hinder strategic decision-making. Strategic decisions involve a holistic view of the present and future, considering not only the immediate steps but also the potential impact on our overarching aspirations. Myopic goals, unfortunately, can limit our strategic thinking. Long-term success often involves a dance between persistence and adaptability. Myopic goals, however, may lean too heavily towards persistence at the cost of adaptability. Flexibility in our goals and decisions allows us to navigate the twists and turns of life, adjusting our course while staying true to our broader vision.

The key is finding a balance – maintaining clarity in our goals while allowing flexibility in our approach. It's like having a destination in mind but being open to alternative routes that might lead to unexpected discoveries. This balance empowers us to make decisions that not only propel us towards immediate goals but also contribute to sustained, long-term success.

Chapter 8

Redefining Success

Let's dive into a journey of reimagining success, challenging the conventional beliefs that often paint it as an unrelenting climb without room for pauses or shifts. What if success isn't a fixed destination but a dynamic, ever-changing landscape? In this narrative, quitting becomes a pivotal aspect, not as a sign of defeat but as a strategic move in the orchestration of our unique version of success. Picture success not as a rigid summit but as a fluid, personal journey. What if quitting is not a setback but a discerning choice, an acknowledgment that the path we embarked upon might not align with our evolving vision? Think of quitting not as surrendering but as a deliberate step toward a truer sense of success.

It's a recognition that some paths are dead ends, and quitting becomes the compass guiding us towards a more authentic journey.

Traditional success narratives resist change, presenting persistence as unwavering virtue. But in this redefined narrative, success thrives on adaptability. Quitting becomes a tool for embracing change, a willingness to pivot when the journey demands a different direction.

Explore the paradox of quitting, challenging the notion that it equates to short-term failure. Quitting strategically can be the compass guiding us toward long-term success. It's an acknowledgment that quitting certain endeavors opens the door to uncharted territories and new opportunities.

Success, in this context, is not just about reaching predefined goals but about cultivating a better tomorrow. Quitting becomes a conscious choice to reallocate energy towards endeavors that authentically align with our values and aspirations. Traditionally, success can feel like a societal cage of external validation. Redefining success liberates us. Quitting becomes a declaration of autonomy, a courageous step towards a success narrative that is uniquely ours. In challenging conventional notions, we paint a picture of holistic success. Success is not just about professional achievements but also about personal fulfillment, well-being, and genuine happiness. Quitting, in this perspective, becomes a tool for sculpting a life that resonates with our truest desires.

Let's talk about the liberating power of letting go, a journey filled with the courage to release the weight of the past in pursuit of a brighter future. It's not just an action; it's an embrace of freedom, a daring step into the unknown, and a commitment to creating space for what lies ahead. Letting go is more than a decision; it's an embrace of liberation. It's choosing to untangle ourselves from the knots of the past, opening ourselves to the promise of new beginnings. It takes courage, a willingness to step into uncertainty with open arms. Our past can sometimes feel like a heavy load. Letting go is the art of shedding that weight, recognizing that our history doesn't define our future. It's a brave act of releasing the anchors that tie us to what no longer contributes to our growth. Letting go is like clearing out space for the future. It's wiping the slate clean, allowing room for fresh experiences, unexplored paths, and the countless possibilities that a better tomorrow holds. It's about making room for the new strokes of our evolving narrative.

Far from a sign of weakness, letting go is a testament to resilience. It's understanding that life is a continuous dance of change, and our strength lies in our ability to adapt. Resilience emerges from the acknowledgment that letting go isn't a loss but a transformative process.

Letting go is stepping bravely into the unknown, a leap of faith fueled by the belief that what awaits is more fulfilling than what we leave behind. It's an act of trust – in ourselves and in the inherent beauty of new beginnings. Letting go becomes a journey into uncharted territories, driven by a sense of adventure. Far from being an endpoint, letting go is a prelude to growth. It's about evolving beyond our past selves, shedding old layers to reveal the resilience beneath. Letting go propels us forward, lighting the way toward a future where our authenticity can flourish and where personal growth becomes a continuous journey.

In the process of letting go, we discover parts of ourselves previously hidden. It's a journey of self-discovery, acknowledging that our true essence is not confined by past choices or circumstances. Letting go liberates us to explore our authenticity, guiding us toward a future aligned with our genuine aspirations.

Chapter 9

Lessons from Forced Quitting

Let's explore the profound insights drawn from experiences where quitting was not a choice but a necessity – a journey that unveils the resilience and growth born from the crucible of forced quitting. In these narratives, we discover that sometimes, the most transformative lessons arise from circumstances that compel us to redirect our paths.

In some chapters of our lives, quitting is not a voluntary decision but a necessity thrust upon us. These moments become crucibles of transformation, where the fire of necessity tests our resilience, pushing us to adapt and evolve in ways we might not have imagined.

Forced quitting propels us into uncharted waters, demanding that we abandon the familiar and confront the unknown. It's a journey of uncertainty, where the compass of our choices is recalibrated. In these uncharted territories, we often discover facets of ourselves – strengths, resilience, and adaptability – that might have remained dormant in the absence of such challenges. Resilience is not merely a concept; it is a quality forged in the crucible of adversity. Forced quitting becomes the anvil where resilience is shaped and honed. It's in these moments of facing the unexpected that we tap into reservoirs of inner strength we may not have known existed. Adaptation is the ally of forced quitting. It's the art of not merely surviving but thriving in the face of change. The growth that emerges is often a result of our ability to adapt – to reevaluate, redirect, and emerge stronger on the other side of circumstances that might have otherwise seemed insurmountable.

Forced quitting challenges our perspectives. It compels us to reassess our goals, values, and priorities. What initially appears as a setback may, in hindsight, reveal itself as a pivotal moment that redirected our trajectory towards a more fulfilling path.

In the crucible of forced quitting, we assemble a toolkit of coping mechanisms. These tools become invaluable in navigating the uncertainties of life. From resilience to adaptability, from the courage to embrace change to the wisdom to discern new opportunities – each forced quitting experience contributes to refining our toolkit for future challenges. Forced quitting often feels like an unplanned detour. However, it's in these detours that we encounter unexpected vistas, encounter diverse experiences, and forge connections that contribute to the richness of our life journey. Embracing the detour becomes a lesson in finding beauty and growth amid unexpected twists.

In hindsight, a life woven with forced quitting experiences reveals a tapestry enriched with unexpected threads. Each thread symbolizes a lesson, a moment of resilience, or a burst of personal growth. These experiences, though initially unwelcome, contribute to the intricate beauty of our life story.

Conclusion

As we wrap up this journey delving into the intricate dance of quitting, it feels like we're standing at a crossroads, surrounded by the echoes of resilience, newfound wisdom, and the promise of fresh beginnings. This exploration wasn't just about quitting; it was a deep dive into self-discovery, growth, and the audacity to shape a life that genuinely feels like our own.

In these chapters, we've unraveled the paradoxes of quitting, faced losses, confronted identity dilemmas, and weighed the costs of opportunities. Through these revelations, the resounding truth emerged – quitting isn't a mark of weakness but a strategic and courageous move toward a better tomorrow, a realization that the path forward might involve detours and recalibrations. Forced quitting, that uninvited companion on our life's journey, revealed itself not as an adversary but as a catalyst for transformation. In the crucible of necessity, we discovered an innate resilience capable of weathering the unexpected, adapting to change, and emerging stronger in the face of adversity. Our exploration guided us through the realms of self-discovery, where we challenged the conventional notions of success, redefined our goals, and embraced the liberating power of letting go. Through these revelations, we've woven a narrative inviting us to reconsider not just quitting but our entire approach to navigating life's complexities.

As we say goodbye to these pages, let's carry forward the wisdom gained from examining quitting in all its facets. Let's be architects of our destiny, unconfined by societal expectations or fear of judgment. May our decisions be guided by the compass of authenticity, the courage to embrace change, and the understanding that quitting, when wielded with discernment, is a tool for sculpting a life aligned with our deepest aspirations.

In the grand tapestry of our existence, quitting is not an endpoint; it's a brushstroke contributing to the evolving masterpiece of our lives. So, let's embark on the next chapter with purpose, a reservoir of resilience, and the unwavering belief that in knowing when to quit, we empower ourselves to shape a future that reflects the truest essence of who we are. As these final notes linger, may they resonate as a melody of empowerment, echoing the possibility of a life lived authentically, courageously, and with the boundless potential that unfolds when we embrace the art of quitting.

Leaving a Review

Dear Reader,

I hope you're doing well. I want to express my sincere thanks for choosing to explore the contents of this book. The journey has been exceptional, and I genuinely hope you found the book both enlightening and valuable.

As an author, your feedback means a lot to me. I would be grateful if you could take a moment to share your thoughts and impressions by leaving a review on the platform where you obtained the book.

Your review not only offers valuable insights for me but also acts as a guide for other readers who may be contemplating whether this book suits their needs and interests. Whether it's a brief comment or a more detailed reflection, your honest feedback is highly valued.

Thank you once again for being part of this literary journey. I eagerly anticipate hearing your thoughts and sincerely appreciate the time and consideration you invest in this.

Best regards,

Lane J. Taylor